The Call

Miriam Hellman

Prophetic Ministries

2013 Que Street, NW, Washington, DC 20009 (202) 265-4249

<u>**The Call**</u>

ISBN 1-891309-06-4

Published by:
Prophetic Ministries
2013 Que Street, NW,
Washington, DC 20009
(202) 265-4249

Other books by Miriam Hellman:

God and the gods, Travelers from Another World
Why Blood? The Highest Sacrifice
The Power of the Endless Blessing
The Prosperous Soul
Signs and Wonders
Sealed for the Battle
Ministry - A Way of Life
The Seer
Offense

Books can be ordered from Prophetic Ministries.

All Scripture quotations are taken from the Authorized King James Version of the Bible.

The Call

Table of Contents

About the Cover

The cover of this book is the picture of a beautiful flower called the iris. I have chosen this cover picture to convey a spiritual message from the scriptures about the theme of this book - the meaning and fulfillment of the call of God upon your life.

The word "iris" is the Greek word used for the rainbow found in the Book of Revelation. Above the throne of God, the rainbow depicts the Alpha and the Omega of God, the judgment and mercy of God in all ages, the beginning and the end of all spectrums of God's work and purposes found in the Bible.

The iris is also the seeing part of the eye. The one who possesses vision sees what is before his eye. I trust that this book, entitled <u>*The Call,*</u> *will be an eye-opener to divine and practical insights that will help you to fulfill your call as God leads you by His Holy Spirit.*

"Where there is no vision, the people perish:
but he that keepeth the law, happy is he."
(Proverbs 29:18)

"... for many be called,
but few chosen."
(Matthew 20:16)

Chapter 1

Are You Prepared to be Called?

If you realize that you are called of God to be a minister for the Lord Jesus Christ, this means that you will be different from others in many respects. The implications of these differences mean that others will also think that you are different.

Are you prepared to be different?

This is an essential question that must be resolved within the heart and mind of the "called vessel" which will determine your usefulness to the Lord. Yielding your will and your ways to Him for His will and His ways to be brought forth will determine how He uses you in the ministry He has ordained for you.

Because human nature wants to be homogenized, to be like everyone else, we find ourselves despising being different, not wanting others to think we are odd. However, history bears the record that a born leader - or a born again minister of the Gospel - is truly different from the norm.

In the church we find two kinds of ministries exhibited. One type is comprised of those individuals who are basically taught the Bible and taught how to be ministers by men. The other type of minister is one who is raised up by the Holy Ghost. This kind of ministry has been taught by God, and has come into a revelation of ministry by the teaching anointing of the Holy Spirit.

The question may be asked, is it wrong to be taught by a man? The answer most assuredly is no. For even those who are taught by the revelation of God are also placed by Him under earthly tutors until the time appointed of the Father (Galatians 4:2).

Nevertheless, there is a major difference in the spiritual ability exhibited by the one who has sought and received the Holy Spirit as his teacher, and the minister who has received the majority of his teaching from other men's revelations. Jesus said,

"Howbeit when he, the Spirit of truth, is come, he will guide you into all truth: for he shall not speak of himself; but whatsoever he shall hear, that shall he speak: and he will shew you things to come." (John 16:13)

It is most important for those that are called to the ministry to understand ministry. It is of paramount importance that one be able to rightly divide the Word of Truth, so that instruction in the body of Christ may increase advancement rather than disperse confusion. I John 2:27 states,

"But the anointing which ye have received of him abideth in you, and ye need not that any man teach you: but as the same anointing teacheth you of all things, and is truth, and is no lie, and even as it hath taught you, ye shall abide in him."

Does this mean we do not need instruction? No, it means that if you sense deep within you that God wants to use you in a profound way and you desire to be used in this way, then the Holy Ghost will become your teacher. This in no way eliminates the need for Bible schools and ministry training grounds, and the other "God raised up" resources that we are so fortunate to have available to us, but as ministers in the making, we approach those resources not as our sole teachers, knowing that God Himself will teach us in the way He chooses (Psalms 25:12).

The office of the teacher is one of the most important ministry gifts to the body of Christ. For the man or woman who is called and anointed by God as a teacher in the body of Christ has the ministry of the teacher, the Holy Spirit, in manifestation in him as he instructs God's people. In this sense, when the true teaching gift is in operation, the Holy Spirit is the teacher, and not the man.

I know many times out of much personal experience, that while preaching or teaching, I am amazed at the words of wisdom and the greatness of the grace of God that proceeds from a true Holy Spirit utterance. I find myself more often than not to be among those being instructed, even though it is through my voice that the Holy Spirit makes His message or His instruction known.

The greatest example of the teacher is Jesus. He was, as His disciples called Him, the Master. For these men, this was the same as being taught of God. Jesus chose the twelve apostles; they did not choose Him, neither did they join His ministry as some join ministries today, looking for new job opportunities.

These disciples were called by Jesus to join with Him to accomplish the things that the Father had given Him to do, and to have a lasting part in His ministry. Their taking their part in His ministry began the instruction that would be necessary to equip them for their respective ministries which would follow at a later time. As the apostles worked continually with Jesus, they were always being instructed under His leadership. We must realize that there is no end to the instruction that we all need, which will continue on even into heaven.

Chapter 2

The Church
Man's Way or God's Way

Jesus emerges from the pages of Jewish history as a Rabbi or teacher whose understanding of God and His methods was inconsistent with the religious framework of His day. He was viewed by the spiritual leaders of His time to be outside of their system of understanding the way in which God was to be pleased and approached. Though viewed as outside of the system, yet He was not outside of the way that was ordained by God, for He said concerning Himself, *"I am the way, the truth, and the life: no man cometh unto the Father, but by me"* (John 14:6).

We know Jesus as the founder, the formulator, and the head of the Church. In Judaism, the place of worship in the nation was the temple which resided in Jerusalem, the city of the great King. But in every neighborhood throughout the nation there was a synagogue for the teaching of the scripture and tradition.

Jesus is the head of the Church and the sound of the Church. Church by definition means the assembling of the believers. Jesus as the head chose disciples that He personally trained in the ways of God, in the truths of the scriptures. Had they remained a part of the Judeo system of their day and not followed Jesus, they never would have borne the title "Apostle." When they became a part of Jesus' ministry, the joining was total and complete. It was for their instruction, their perfection, and for the purposes of God.

In their yieldedness to the ways of Jesus, they came to recognize the wisdom of God and the purpose for their lives. They understood that through joining their lives to Jesus and working with Him, everything they were going to receive would come in and through His ministry. They did not seek to obtain their instruction or the fulfillment of their needs in various other places.

I want to share something about the ministry of Lester Sumrall. Lester Sumrall joined himself with Howard Carter many years ago, and he knew within his heart what God called him to do. He was not persuaded by the persuasions of men. This is what gave him such an extraordinary career in God: he did not receive his instruction - don't misunderstand this - in a local church. He would not be what God meant him to be, sitting in a local church. He would have been finished with a local commitment and decision. He committed himself to what he knew deep inside of him was the call of God and the cry of the Spirit for the earth. And he set out to follow Howard Carter who said, "I'm going, and if you have the money, you catch up with me. ***I'm not waiting for you.***"

There were times when Lester Sumrall didn't have the money and Howard Carter left without him. Howard Carter said, "Believe God for yourself." No church took up a collection for Lester Sumrall to fulfill his missions career. He had to make the personal decisions for his ministry. He didn't even know where he was going, but he found the destinations in the Spirit and went on to spearhead a movement. He ***shook*** nations like the Philippines with such deliverances from demons that are unparalleled with anything most of us know about. He really had the ministry of delivering the Gadarene demoniac.

Why? Because he heard the call of the Spirit and he knew where his call could be developed without compromise. The moment a man compromises with his call, he is unprepared in the spirit and it becomes obvious to all men that he is unprepared. Then he is finished, because divided commitments and divided visions collapse all preparation.

I am not an expert on Lester Sumrall's life, but I remember this story from the early days of my Christianity because it impressed me in the spirit. I want to be impressed by people who have made impressions on the earth. I am not impressed with ministers who make no impressions on the earth, but only seek to please men. They are not developers of ministries, they do not bear fruit in the kingdom of God, and they are not able to reproduce after their own kind.

Paul produced ministers after his own kind. Jesus produced ministries after His own kind. Take a look at the kind of person you are. If what you see is what you want to be for the rest of your life, that is what you will be.

Chapter 3

Learning the Ways of God

The most important part of the learning process in the development of a minister is in learning the ways of God. This may not be so easily seen or understood at first glance, if one reads the scripture casually. For example, in the Gospel of Matthew, Chapter 28, we read an account of the resurrection of Jesus from the dead. We learn that the first person who saw Jesus after He had risen was Mary Magdalene.

We also learn that before seeing Jesus, she spoke with an angel who said to her,

> *"He is not here: for he is risen, as he said. Come, see the place where the Lord lay. And go quickly, and tell his disciples that he is risen from the dead; and behold, he goeth before you into Galilee; there shall ye see him: lo, I have told you."* (Matthew 28:6-7)

It was a woman who was first given the honor and the command to tell Jesus' disciples that He had risen from the dead and instructed them to go to another city to meet Him. This amazing truth is often pointed out in Bible school, but sadly goes unrecognized even in the church of the 20th century.

Many women with the call of God upon their lives to be proclaimers and preachers of the resurrection of Jesus are still wrestling within themselves with unsettled questions of whether or not a woman can be called into the ministry. Yet, ***it was God's way*** to send the women first with this message. These women were called upon to execute a heavenly assignment. They were instructed by the angel to tell the disciples, who did not even believe that Jesus had risen from the dead, that they were to meet Him in Galilee.

Think about this. These are some of the ways of God revealed in the Bible. Jesus was crucified in Jerusalem, and there He arose from the dead. Now, if you were Jesus, and you arose from the dead in Jerusalem, and all your people were frightened because of their association with you, and you knew they were there, would you not go to them in this place of their distress? Why would your people have to meet you in another city? The natural man says, "It's right here; this is my place. I do not have to go anywhere. God can meet me here."

It is not God's way to do things in that manner. The way of the natural man is not inevitably the way of the Lord. As we read the Bible, we see that God chooses and determines our meeting places. He ordains the meeting place that will take us to higher and holy ground. He often sends us to a place of His choosing, because He cannot do a thing with us where we are.

I always thought it amazing that the disciples had to go all the way to Galilee, when Jesus arose from the tomb in Jerusalem. Everything had to be in place for the next great event that was to take place in Jerusalem: Pentecost. When Jesus sent word that He would meet them in Galilee, Peter, James, John and the others did not have an angelic visitation bidding them on their way, they instead had a woman sent to them - a woman with a message and an instruction.

God often wants to send us someplace else to have a meeting. This is what we call a "divine appointment." What if the disciples had not kept the appointment in Galilee? Then they would not have been given the subsequent appointment in Jerusalem on the Day of Pentecost. Divine appointments are stepping stones in our pilgrims' progress on into eternity.

This is a very important lesson. The disciples understood after Jesus' death that they were in political danger. They were by themselves, and they were outside of the covering of the synagogue. They had joined themselves with Jesus, and He was their all in all. Now, Jesus is gone from their midst and no angel appears to them.

But an angel tells a woman to go to the disciples and tell them Jesus will meet them in Galilee.

> *And as they went to tell his disciples, behold, Jesus met them, saying, All hail. And they came and held him by the feet, and worshipped him. Then said Jesus unto them, Be not afraid: go tell my brethren that they go into Galilee, and there shall they see me.*
>
> (Matthew 28:9-10)

This is a message for ministry. Just as there are two kinds of ministers, those taught of God or taught of men, so there are also, within those frameworks, calls to the local body and calls to the universal body.

Local vision is to a small segment of the body of Christ, and universal vision is to the whole body of Christ. First, it is for you to know to what vision you are called, and what it is you are called to do.

If you are called to make tapes, by all means, make those tapes. If you are called to work in Children's Church, by all means, be in Children's Church. If you are called to be a care leader in a local church, by all means, be a care leader in a local church. But if you are called to the universal church, then by all means, live in that call. There is no merit in trying to make yourself what you are not. You must be in your place in the body of Christ, as all of your fulfillment will be connected to what you are called to do.

Chapter 4

How Does a Man Know What He is Called To Do?

How does a man know what he is called to do? He knows by his giftings and he knows by his heart.

There is a woman connected with our ministry who met us several years ago. One day God spoke to her the word, "Cairo." Just this word. Days later, she went into a Christian bookstore and overheard people talking about my Prophetic Ministries' Praise and Worship Conference in Egypt. God allowed us to have the first Praise and Worship Conference that had ever taken place in Egypt, which enabled the church in the Middle East, for the first time, to know the different aspects and dimensions of praise, worship, and glory. She knew instantly in her heart that this praise and worship conference was the ministry vehicle God would use to get her to Cairo. She inquired where Prophetic Ministries met, came to one meeting, and signed up for the ministry tour to Egypt and Israel.

When she joined us on the tour, we were not sure if she was unhappy or not that she had paid her money for what she was experiencing. She looked so serious and didn't say a word. We would say among ourselves, "What do you think about that lady? Do you think this is too much for her?" But then, as we drove into Galilee through the Jordan Valley, (the Beka as they call it), there is a certain narrow place in the road where you cross the Jordan River. There is a tiny bridge with just room enough for one vehicle at a time. In this place, she stood up and told about her ancestors as slaves and how they sang about the Jordan.

Then, I asked the bus driver to stop the bus, and this woman who had not said a word sang, "Roll, Jordan, Roll!" I thought, "Oh, my goodness; all of this is inside this little lady." But you see, this is an example of how "calls" are brought forth by the Spirit. They come forth in unusual ways. One word is spoken, and the steps of a righteous man are ordered by the Lord into a Christian bookstore.

You hear a conversation, you don't know anything about the people, but the lady at the counter says, "Oh, go to the meeting. Miriam is a great teacher; you'll enjoy it." You go, sign up, give your check, and oh, my goodness! She signed up for much more. She signed up for her life's call.

Many experience conflicts in their hearts and in their minds concerning what they are called to do, and why the call of God upon their lives never seems to come forth. Many times my heart goes out to certain individuals in the body of Christ that I see seeking recognition, and I know it will never come.

Does this mean there is something wrong with those people or their pastors for not recognizing them? The answer is no! If I was in a local church and the local church did not recognize me, and I was not progressing in what I was called to do, I would know it was not the devil, and I would know that it was not the fault of the ministry. I would realize that God was trying to tell me something else, and that I was the one who was dull of perception.

Why should we think that it is acceptable to be in the wrong place for the wrong reason, and still think that we will be developed? Is this the fault of the people in the body? No, it is the fault of the person who is unable to know in his heart when a particular body is not the place for his development.

Chapter 5

Coming to Your Christian Senses

We have to have Elijah sense.

We know very little concerning the life of Elijah. He was a mystery person. The Bible gives no information concerning his background or his family. Of the other prophets it is said, "Jeremiah, son of Hilkiah" and so on. Background is given to tell where most of the prophets came from, but all we know about Elijah is that he was a Tishbite, and we don't even know what that means.

But we know that he emerges on the pages of history, from out of nowhere, and is used as a prophet to the nation. He is a one man nation-shaker.

Elijah, a one man nation-shaker, was not part and parcel of the local synagogue system where the politics of Jezebel and Ahab prevailed. Where man's systems prevail, "so doth the politics."

If you are a real history-maker or world-shaker, you never involve yourself with church politics or people pleasing. The outstanding men and women in the Bible were outstanding because they believed wholeheartedly the words and directions of God. Their ears were not bent towards human understanding as to how things were to be made successful.

I have yet to find a history-maker or world-shaker in man's system in the Bible. We are not talking about being opposed. We are talking about calls, especially calls to the universal body.

Do you hear the call?

Chapter 6

Breaking Through into the Call

Do you believe that Jesus is coming, and that this is the generation that will see Him? He is not going to come until the harvest is reaped. Do you know how few laborers there are? It is beyond imagination how few! Are you going to "shake" the nations?

When you hear about four or five other ministers who are making an impact on nations, do you think those few are going to do it all? It is going to take many shakers, many apostles, many evangelists. It is going to take many pastors to pick up the work of those ministries. Every one of the five-fold ministries will have to experience an explosion in call and office.

There will have to come an explosion, in the spiritual realm, of true shepherds. This must be. But there will never be shepherds if there are no sheep. Now, we have thirty different local churches in every city. But we have no explosion in the multiplication of sheep. We have no harvest if we do not have apostolic ministries, prophetic ministries, and evangelistic ministries. These are the ministries that shake the nations. These are the ministries that shake hell. These are the ministries that plunder hell and populate heaven, and we need an explosion of these ministries.

Most people sit in their churches saying, "God hasn't called me to do such things." But I maintain instead, that they have not had the ear to hear the call. It is very easy to abdicate the responsibility of being called into the labor of the harvest by pleading deafness. Spiritual handicaps relieve people from world commitments and make it easy for them to sit back and leave the responsibility to someone with a hearing ear.

This spiritual insight can be best understood in the words of Isaiah who said,

Also I heard the voice of the Lord, saying, Whom shall I send, and who will go for us? Then said I, Here am I; send me. And he said, Go, and tell this people, Hear ye indeed, but understand not; and see ye indeed, but perceive not. Make the heart of this people fat, and make their ears heavy, and shut their eyes; lest they see with their eyes, and hear with their ears, and understand with their heart, and convert, and be healed. (Isaiah 6:8-10)

These indeed are very sobering thoughts.

Without the preparation in the life of the person, there is no ministry. What we will have is more pastors pastoring people who have been making the rounds of the churches. We find more people choose the ministry of pastor because they see that it is a ministry that brings security through tithes. In ministries like my own, you have to trust God, not a tithe. So few people are willing to be prepared.

Some people do sense the need for preparation, but then, unfortunately, there is no one to help them. You cannot go into these ministry positions unless you are instructed and discipled, not as in past discipleship training where people told you who to marry and whether you ate grapefruit or oranges for breakfast, and what you did in your spare time. Jesus trained his disciples. He made them into the same kind of minister that He was.

Without discipleship, it is impossible for these ministries to come into existence and it is impossible for them to be developed in one's life. Lester Sumrall would not be what he is today were it not for the Holy Ghost and Howard Carter. And R.W. Schambach would not be what he is today if it had not been for A. A. Allen. You can go down the line and see that every person who made a mark on history was discipled. This person was present every time there was an opportunity to learn from the mentor. The commitment was present, the anointing came on them, and the apostolic, the evangelistic and the prophetic calls were perpetuated. When that link is broken, there is an incredible breakdown in the entire system.

The local church is a part of the universal church. The major work of the local body is designed for the care and nourishing of the flock. The care of the flock is an important commitment that the pastor accepts from God. Care is important, and we don't want breakdowns in this area. There are breakdowns in the church when we have people in pastoral positions who are not true pastors, but call themselves pastors. Shepherds who are not shepherds. I love what Ezekiel says:

> 1. *And the word of the Lord came unto me, saying,*
> 2. *Son of man, prophesy against the shepherds of Israel, prophesy, and say unto them, Thus saith the Lord God unto the shepherds; Woe be to the shepherds of Israel that do feed themselves! should not the shepherds feed the flocks?*
> 3. *Ye eat the fat, and ye clothe you with the wool, ye kill them that are fed: but ye feed not the flock.*
> 4. *The diseased have ye not strengthened, neither have ye healed that which was sick, neither have ye bound up that which was broken, neither have ye brought again that which was driven away, neither have ye sought that which was lost; but with force and with cruelty have ye ruled them.*
> 5. *And they were scattered, because there is no shepherd: and they became meat to all the beasts of the field, when they were scattered.*

6. *My sheep wandered through all the mountains, and upon every high hill: yea, my flock was scattered upon all the face of the earth, and none did search or seek after them.*
7. *Therefore, ye shepherds, hear the word of the Lord;*
8. *As I live, saith the Lord God, surely because my flock became a prey, and my flock became meat to every beast of the field, because there was no shepherd, neither did my shepherds search for my flock, but the shepherds fed themselves, and fed not my flock;*
9. *Therefore, O ye shepherds, hear the word of the Lord;*
10. *Thus saith the Lord God; Behold, I am against the shepherds; and I will require my flock at their hand and cause them to cease from feeding the flock; neither shall the shepherds feed themselves any more; for I will deliver my flock from their mouth, that they may not be meat for them.*

(Ezekiel 34:1-10)

So, we cannot have a breakdown in any ministerial area.

Elijah was a man who was taught of God. Wouldn't we all like to have such a ministry? Do you think that his ministry suffered because he didn't go to church three times a week, and to Bible Study and every church meeting? How did he get such a ministry without doing all those things? The answer is simple. He was not inclined to religious thinking, as most people are. He was not inclined to believe that his call and success were dependent solely on his religious activities and reliance on attending meetings.

His success was that his ear was inclined unto God's word, and his heart was inclined unto God's ways.

> *My son, attend to my words; incline thine ear unto my sayings. Let them not depart from thine eyes; keep them in the midst of thine heart. For they are life unto those that find them, and health to all their flesh.* (Proverbs 4:20-22)

People with religious spirits are totally wedded to the religious systems. This is not a message to be a loner, or to separate yourself from the body of Christ. In fact, the Word states that in this day we should not forsake the assembling of the elect. No, I am just saying that Elijah had such a ministry because he was taught of God.

Even after Elijah shook the nation, he was in trouble. I have always been thrilled by this verse in the book of James, that Elijah was a man of "like passions" as ourselves.

He prayed that it not rain and it didn't rain. And he prayed that it rain and it rained. But, he was a man of like passions (James 5:17-18). In fact, most of the people in the Bible who were used in the greatest way experienced the greatest personal failures in their lives.

Isn't it wonderful? It ought to be encouraging to everyone that no one is failure proof. Only Jesus is infallible. No other man was ever infallible. The calls of so many people have suffered because they failed, or made a terrible mistake and were never able to recoup themselves.

It is important to understand that if you have had a failure or made a bad mistake in your life - if you have fallen trap to passion and did something terrible - no person is fully able to help you out of that. Only the Lord can help you fully, for it is He who wants you to see what you are made of. Your call and your mistake are tied up in your relationship with God, and He and He alone is able to correct your mistake properly and get you back on track. If you are not able to receive His correction and His instruction as only He can give you, then you are just plainly not ministry material.

Elijah is seen calling down fire from heaven, and killing the false prophets of Baal. This is a big execution order. This is a superman of sorts; he has them all killed. Do you know how many prophets they say were there? Hundreds of them! Yet, he has them all killed in one day. That is a true expression of holy boldness, isn't it?

However, the next day Elijah receives a message from Jezebel:

> 2. *Then Jezebel sent a messenger unto Elijah, saying, So let the gods do to me, and more also, if I make not thy life as the life of one of them by tomorrow about this time.*
> 3. *And when he saw that, he arose, and went for his life, and came to Beersheba, which belongeth to Judah, and left his servant there.*
> 4. *But he himself went a day's journey into the wilderness, and came and sat down under a juniper tree: and he requested for himself that he might die; and said, It is enough; now, O Lord, take away my life; for I am not better than my fathers.* (I Kings 19:2-4)

I think this passage is wonderful. These things encourage me. Some people like to hear "The Lord is my shepherd ..." I would rather read something like this, because many times, if you have a call to ministry, you need a different kind of message as an encouragement, such as, "The Lord is my Master. The Lord is my Manager. The Lord is my Director."

Many times, we would just like to die and forget it, because believe me, every call of God is tested to the final degree. You will be tested. Your family will test you. Your church will test you. Your friends will test you. Your finances will test you. Your strength will test you. Things that happen will test you, and things that don't happen will test you. When nothing seems to be happening, it is a big test - a major test.

And so we continue to read in the chapter that Elijah just went into a cave. He came hither to a cave and lodged there. He hid in a cave. There are lots of people who just want to hide in themselves. This is what the cave is. It is called "cave in." Men ought always to pray and not faint. And behold, the word of the Lord came unto him and He said to him, "What in the world are you doing here? Who told you you could cave in? Who gave you permission to cave in?"

I want to go back to the beginning of the chapter and look at exactly what happened after Elijah's high point. I would describe it in these words: ***he was threatened***.

There are people reading this with great calls of God upon their lives. Not little calls, ***great*** calls. And I say to you in ministry, you will be eternally responsible whether or not you submitted yourself to God for this call. Your choices will be judged eternally. This is a serious thing.

Elijah was threatened. There are things that threaten ministries and things that threaten ministers. What things are we afraid of? Most fears involve other people. They are the biggest threat - what other people think of us, how they understand us, how they perceive us, what they say concerning us, and their critique of what we are supposed to do.

So the Lord said, "What are you doing here, Elijah?"

Elijah said, "I've been very jealous for the Lord of Hosts. The children of Israel have forsaken thy covenant. I'm the only one."

And the Lord said, "Go forth and stand in the mountain before the Lord."

And Elijah goes. You know the rest of what happened. The Lord was not in the earthquake, and the

Lord was not in the wind, but the Lord was in the still, small voice.

Elijah had been given a prior instruction. And the Lord said, "Now just get going and get back on the path that I originally sent you in. You have no right to deviate from the call. You have no right to deviate."

The first time we deviate from the call because we feel threatened, we are already on the wrong road. It is wonderful that these things are written for our instruction. Elijah caved in. What threatens you? What threatens your call? You have got to settle it. Do not cave in!

Chapter 7

Recognizing the Gift, Not the Man

We read in the Bible that when Jesus arose from the dead, He gave gifts unto men. And some were apostles, some were prophets, and some were pastors, teachers and evangelists. He gave these ministries as gifts to the world. A ministry call means that your life exists for the blessing and edification of other people. A ministry gift is not for you. A minister's call is the gift of God.

I am talking specifically about the five-fold ministry. In these ministries, if one is called to be a pastor, he is going to learn his call best from an anointed shepherd. He is not going to learn it from an evangelist. He is not going to learn it from an apostle. He is going to learn it through observing an excellent pastoral model.

We are incomplete without the five-fold ministry gifts. If you know that your shaping is going to come in and through the local body of Christ, then you are to remain there. But if you are called to be an evangelist, you are not going to get that development from a captain of twenty or fifty. This will not be a correct development model for your call. Your lack of understanding will totally undercut your call.

It is a lack of understanding that causes people to say, "It was prophesied to me that I'm an apostle or prophet." No one ever prophesied to Paul that he would one day be a prophet. But, Jesus did ***outline*** to Paul what he would do. He did not begin as a prophet, but he was taught of God.

Paul frequently went to the synagogue to preach Jesus, but there his message was not received. Hence, after repeated times of being refused and thrown out of the synagogue, he understood the words of Isaiah, who prophesied that Israel would neither have eyes nor ears to receive their salvation. And so, Paul realized that a change would have to come into his ministry, and that he would take the message of salvation through Jesus Christ to the non-Jewish world. He then became the first apostle to the Gentile nations in fulfillment of the words that Jesus spoke to him when He appeared to him.

This is a perfect example to show all of us that we frequently need to grow and mature in the understanding of what the Lord speaks to us concerning the ministry He has called us to. So often we try to understand with our mind what the Lord is trying to say to us, when truly only the Holy Spirit can enlighten the eyes of our understanding (Ephesians 1:18).

When Paul sought fellowship, the Bible says he went to the apostles. He did not seek his major fellowship beneath his ministry call. He sought fellowship among the apostles. Then, after he and Barnabus traveled awhile, they came back and told the rest of the apostles what they were doing.

A major part of your instruction is going to come through fellowship with people of the same call and beliefs. If you step into lower fellowship, not just lower, but different, you are severely hindering your call. You cannot afford it!

In the Acts of the Apostles, Chapter 2, it is wonderful to read about the early church, but we have to have the courage to have THE church. I cannot think locally because I am not placed locally in the body of Christ. Yet I have a relationship with a local body.

I remember the first time I went into my church. It was the first time I saw the glory of God manifested in a service, and I saw a ministry that was not only serving people locally, but reaching the world. I saw that God placed me where I could be developed fully to fulfill the call of God upon my life, because my pastor is an apostle and a prophet. Does that mean he is not a pastor? No, it means that he is a pastor and more than a pastor. I am not a pastor as such, but I do pastor those whom God has placed under my leadership and care.

Ninety percent of the people in my church family are in full-time ministry, evangelizing all over the world. This should not be an unusual thing. On any Sunday, many of the members may not be present - they could likely be in many different parts of the world. All the years I have gone to church, nobody has ever said, "Oh, we missed you."

Do you know what "I missed you" means? It means, "Where were you last Sunday?" Nobody ever says they miss anybody in this manner in our ministry, because it is known that those missing are about their Father's business. In fact, I met my pastor on platforms all over the world last year. The next time I see him, I will see him in Israel. Then, I will probably see him in Florida or someplace else - but probably not in a home church building. I told him he prophesied me right out of the building and into THE church. Hallelujah!

As we continue to read in the Acts of the Apostles, we see that when the church began, it was a threat to what existed in the religious minds of people. A real church is always a threat. The devil threatens ministry gifts so there will not be THE church, because THE church is ordained to destroy the works of the devil.

The real thing is always a threat. If you evoke fear in the enemy, you have succeeded. If you are a threat to the devil, then you know that the Holy Ghost is with you. The apostles turned the world upside down. When they preached, they were told to shut their mouths. They were told by the religious leaders of their day not to preach in the name of Jesus, and to stop stirring up the people. But Peter said to them,

> *"Whether it be right in the sight of God to hearken unto you more than unto God, judge ye. For we cannot but speak the things which we have seen and heard."* (Acts 4:19-20)

When the church is delivered out of prison by angels, then the church has arrived. I do not think we should be denied, or that we should have less of a goal than the model that has been put before us.

Your ministry is only able to be developed to the degree that the model set before you is developed. You will be developed to the extent that the ministry you have put yourself under has been developed. So be very careful what you put yourself under. You will never grow beyond that level.

The kind of man I prefer to look to as a model is John G. Lake. He was never stopped. He got on a boat headed for Africa with his wife, his seven children and no earthly means of support. I often say that those who have money never go to the nations of the world, and those who do not have money, often by faith, are able to go. No doubt, many average churches would have asked him, "Do you think it is right to take a wife and seven children on a boat with no money?" But he just obeyed God.

The passengers had to wait in line to prove that they had a certain amount of money before they were able to depart the boat. John Lake stood in the line without actual money in his pocket, but with faith in his heart. When he got to be about the third person who had to prove he had this sum of money, someone approached him and handed him all that he needed.

When he got off the boat, someone met him and asked, "Are you the missionary that's been sent from America?"

And he said, "Yes."

The person said, "The Lord told me to take you home and take care of you." This person did not hear from any missionary board; they heard from the Holy Ghost.

John Lake went on to do a great apostolic work in Africa, making the REAL church visible before the eyes of the world. There would not have been any revival in Africa today if someone had not been a threat to the devil, if someone had not been discipled by another who was not afraid of the devil.

We will never see our churches filled without the increase and advancement of apostolic ministries. The church in America today seems to have a knack of inhibiting these ministries from coming forth. The apostolic, prophetic, and evangelistic ministries are set in the earth for the increase of the kingdom of God. These are the ministries which are ordained to bring the major increases into the body of Christ. Without the development of the five-fold ministries, we will not see our churches filled.

In the Acts of the Apostles, we read that an angel brought the apostles out of prison, to go right back and stand in public, and start preaching again. This is great! I believe in these days we can also have a decade of destiny, but only for people that sense destiny within. If you study the lives of people who challenged the age in which they lived to change destinies and the course of the world, you find that they experienced unbelievable opposition, and were able to overcome.

In the early Pentecostal movement of the 20th century, the opposition really did throw tomatoes and rotten eggs, but those in the movement just took it and went on. Today as in all times, you become falsely accused, called a variety of derogatory titles, or if you become known you get to be written about in a false manner in a Christian ministry magazine. You can be called a heretic or a sorcerer by a virtual nobody who thinks he is somebody, but we are the ones that are here today, and it is the destiny of this decade that is committed into our hands.

In each generation, the work of God is committed into the hands of that generation. But how are people inspired to go forth if they have no inspiring leader? You have to have a model that inspires. If, instead, you have a model that holds you back, you are finished. You have to have a model that inspires you to go forward. Jesus said simply, *"Go ye into **all** the world, and preach the gospel to every creature"* (Mark 16:15).

"Go ye." You don't need to know as much as you think you need to know. You will learn more in the going and the doing than from listening to a tape series. Now we always recommend our tape series because we think they are the best, and for that, I give God the glory. But I tell you, you can listen to all the tapes in the world, but if you do not have the "go ye" inside of you, what good are the tapes? The tapes are there to inspire you to go. They are there to instruct you to do whatever it is you have to do to see that the call of God upon your life is developed.

And so, the apostles were persecuted, beaten, and forbidden to speak, but they withstood and continued against opposition, to stand in the evil day. They were forbidden to speak, but they stood and continued anyway. Now, just listen to what they prayed:

> *And now, Lord, behold their threatenings: and grant unto thy servants, that with all boldness they may speak thy word, By stretching forth thine hand to heal; and that signs and wonders may be done by the name of thy holy child Jesus.*
> (Acts 4:29-30)

All that gladly received the word preached unto them were baptized and continued steadfastly in the apostles' doctrine (Acts 2:41-42). This is something I do not think we hear too much about. We hear about doctrines, and I believe very much in doctrines. I believe that everything that happens to you in this life and the next is intricately connected to your beliefs, your knowledge, your wisdom, and your understanding in Jesus Christ - the Word of God.

If you are called into the ministry, whatever you believe concerning ministry is most definitely going to affect your success or your failure. Therefore, it is very important that what you believe about ministry be most accurate.

According to the accuracy of your beliefs concerning ministry, so shall your ministry be. If you believe inaccurately concerning ministry, then your ministry will be hindered and will never reach its fullness.

They continued steadfastly. "Continued" is an important word. They did not discontinue, but the newly baptized ***continued*** in apostolic doctrine and fellowship.

Many times I have learned more in fellowship with fellow ministers than I have learned in a church service. To sit down with a minister that is fully developed, seasoned and willing to share, is a priceless experience. You will learn much more out of this kind of fellowship than you will by only going to church. This is what Jesus did. He trained His disciples, sent them out, and corrected them. Then they came home and had the "in-house" meeting.

These were not meetings to discuss how to run the ministry, although I am sure they talked about those things. But these meetings were to discuss the "whys and why nots" of miracles and healings. They were times in which Jesus expounded with greater detail the meanings of the principles of God. They were times of clarifying the meaning of His sayings, and clearing up possible misunderstandings of what He had preached. During these times, the disciples expressed to Jesus freely that they did not fully comprehend the meaning of His words or doctrine. We, as ministers, often need the same kind of in-house meetings to help us over the areas that we are unsure of. Great benefits are derived from fellowship with those who have gone before us, who have like callings as ourselves.

I had a wonderful opportunity to spend part of a day with Brother Hagin. My life changed as a result of that opportunity to fellowship in the deep things of God. One of the fruits of that day is the message "Understanding the Sent One" in my album, *The Sent One*.

There is a difference between one who is sent to minister and one who waits for an invitation to minister. The problem that most beginning ministries have is lack of opportunity for spiritual service. Typically, the new minister/ministry waits to be invited, and the wait may be agonizingly long if there is no recognition, recommendation, or open door forthcoming. Needless to say, this kind of "ministry in waiting" may suffer severe birth pains. However, the Bible looks at ministry opportunity not as a waiting game, but as an issue of choice: a choice either to be sent, or to wait for an invitation.

God had a divine solution for the prophets of old, for instance, in that He did not wait for them to be invited, but rather, sent them on assignments. When we study the ministries of Jesus and His disciples, we see an identical scenario in that they, too, went forward, even though they were never invited even to as much as a local church. Often, in fact, word that Jesus was coming into town preceded Him, and the word was not necessarily one of welcome.

Even so, as in the case of the woman at the well, *"And he must needs go through Samaria."* Although Jesus was not welcome there, His ministry likely beset with harsh, critical accusations, yet the Bible tells us He set His face as a flint.

As ministers of the Gospel, we, like Jesus, may need to go through Samaria, which is the place of spiritual trial, for negotiating both negative and positive environments essential to overall ministry development.

When we look at the evangelistic work of the Apostles Peter and Paul, we see vivid examples of ministries developing in, and through, less than optimal circumstances. These men, who laid the foundation of the church, had ministries based in local house meetings and not in packed-out stadiums. They faced severe trials, discouragements and personal battles to overcome character flaws, but under the hand of the Lord, they became overcomers who preached strong messages and had miracle ministries.

Paul, in particular, became a continuous threat to the devil and, therefore, was continually threatened. Always in the center of controversy, he was never deterred from going on, usually into the next battle. Without these men of substance, and others like them who literally and figuratively "grew up" in the faith, there would be no established church and, consequently, no established pastors.

Chapter 8

The "How" of the Call Realized

In discussing the issue of how a minister of the Gospel is used, I would like to share something that the Lord said to me a few years ago which altered the course of my life and ministry.

One thing that He said to me was this: "Will you allow me to use you the way I want to use you, and not the way you want to be used yourself?"

I answered, "Yes, Lord."

I did not know what I was saying "yes" to, but it did not take long for it to become evident.

This "yes" is not an easy affirmation to give, because we have preconceived ideas of who we are, and personal views of how we want to be used and how we want others to perceive us. But God seems to have a way of using us quite contrary to our nature.

Let me elaborate on this. Although I am aware that personal motivation is a factor, I am opposed to Christian books that instruct according to motivational giftings or natural abilities. Never was a figure in the Bible called or used according to personal motivation. Although the gifts and equipment necessary to the call were resident in those ministers of God, the motivation was not necessarily present, nor the personal perception of their ministry necessarily accurate.

We see this very evidently in the life of Moses. After God called Moses, he had much discussion with the Lord regarding his unsuitability for the task of leading the children of Israel out of bondage. Remember, Moses never set out to be a deliverer. Quite the contrary, he was a premeditated murderer who had committed a crime of passion which forced him to be on the run from the authorities for forty years.

Thank God that Moses was a man of like passions as ourselves, for these are the kinds of people God uses. People who, like Moses, see themselves as unfit, of stammering lips and slow speech. We are all unfit until God enables us.

God did not tell Moses He would instruct him out of a book. He said, *"I will teach your mouth what to say."* And because Moses was the meekest man on earth, he had the ability to be instructed. For contrary to popular thought, meekness is not weakness, but the attribute of one possessed with a great and teachable spirit. God used this teachable man to lead millions of unteachable men out of their captivity.

Jesus tells us that the meek shall inherit the earth. If you want to be a deliverer today, you will be among the meek. For if you can be instructed, you can then ask Jesus for the nations of the world as an inheritance.

The Bible tells us that the children of Israel SAW THE ACTS of God, but Moses KNEW THE MIND of God and knew His ways, because the relationship was made possible by Moses' teachable spirit.

At this point, I would like to relate an important testimony which will shed light on how a call is realized. Years ago, when a well-known minister began his ministry, the thought burned in his heart that he would be the Billy Graham of Bolivia. He sought the Lord in diligent prayer, learned to speak Spanish and went to Bolivia, thoroughly prepared for his first crusade. The fire of evangelism burned within him as he preached, but no one was saved. A second crusade was equally devastating in its failure. He finally admitted defeat and determined he was called to be a pastor. The church he started never numbered very many people, and in spite of continued prayers, the flock never grew and he was, again, devastated.

One day, the Holy Spirit spoke to him from the twelfth chapter of the Book of Romans:

> *I beseech you therefore, brethren, by the mercies of God, that ye present your bodies a living sacrifice, holy, acceptable unto God, which is your reasonable service. And be not conformed to this*

world: but be ye transformed by the renewing of your mind, that ye may prove what is that good, and acceptable, and perfect, will of God. For I say, through the grace given unto me, to every man that is among you, not to think of himself more highly than he ought to think; but to think soberly, according as God hath dealt to every man the measure of faith.

The Lord told him he had concentrated on the first two verses, and had presented his body as a sacrifice and fulfilled the rest of the requisites, but that he had not read far enough. The Lord told him to keep reading and to look at himself soberly.

Today, this minister is a great teacher in the body of Christ, because his call was to teach. He misunderstood. I believe many have misunderstood what God has called them to do, and they will never be happy or fulfilled until they think soberly.

We are not going to save the world if we launch out after being in ministry one month or one year. Because God has dealt to each man a measure of faith, your ministry can proceed only as far as your faith can take you. Be certain, then, to surround yourselves with people who will encourage you in the faith and in your call. I would not want you to be under ministry leadership of one who is afraid to share that ministry, thus leaving you inadequately equipped and underdeveloped.

Seek the will of God and the ways of God, and He will bring you to godly people of like precious faith and similar calls. He will enable you to be aligned with them, to work with them, to cooperate with them, and to be developed in and with and through them, to the glory of God.

Chapter 9

Submission - The Way to Divine Commission

The Oxford Universal Dictionary gives the following definition of the word "submission":

To submit to a spiritual authority means to agree in one's heart to abide by a decision to obey that authority. To submit oneself in conduct and in duty means to bear well even in the midst of differences. It is an act of yielding to the decisions and judgments of another. It is the surrendering of one's will and opinions to aid the will and goal of the leader. It is the ability to humble oneself, and to be always ready in obedience to the head, to place oneself under the control of the person in authority or power. It is the willingness to surrender oneself to judgment, criticism, correction, a condition, treatment, etc. To consent to undergo or abide by a condition. To subject oneself to operations and processes of refining. In the case of a military authority, even to submit oneself to danger for the purpose of victory.

> *See then that ye walk circumspectly, not as fools, but as wise, redeeming the time, because the days are evil. Submitting yourselves one to another in the fear of God.* (Ephesians 5:15-16, 21)

The Word of God exhorts us to give honor where honor is due. Jesus spoke of some in His day saying, "They gave lip service, but not heart service." As ministers, we are to give our best at all times to the minister and ministry God has placed us under, in all ways helping that minister as if you were personally helping Jesus to fulfil the request that He might have asked of you if you had been a part of His earthly ministry.

Many times a novice thinks that he knows best, or that his desires and personal ambitions outweigh his loyalty to his spiritual leader. Jesus said, "He that is faithful in that which is least is faithful also in much. He that is unjust (or holds back) in the least is unjust also in much. If you have not been faithful in that which is another man's, who shall give you that which is your own? No servant can serve two masters, for either he will hate the one, and love the other, or else he will hold to the one and despise the other. You cannot serve God and mammon."

If we are unable to serve another as that one would desire to be served, then we have chosen to be self-serving and this will only hinder the future call of God on your life. This is very evidently seen in the life of David, who served Saul fully and with a pure heart even though Saul's motives and objectives were not right in the sight of God.

One of the greatest examples in the scripture of the greatness that comes into the heart and life of one who truly serves is seen in the life of Joshua.

> *Now after the death of Moses the servant of the Lord it came to pass, that the Lord spake unto Joshua the son of Nun,* ***Moses' minister...*** (Joshua 1:1)

First submit yourself to a true servant of the Lord, then determine to make yourself the minister of that servant. A servant's heart expresses itself by doing those things that the leader desires and which help the leader to move into the greatest spiritual capacity possible. A ministry to another minister puts the other's ministry before their own in every respect. The servant of another ministry, as Joshua was to Moses, puts his heart into the full advancement of that ministry in every way.

Even though the servant may have greater or different abilities in God, at this time he is serving the servant of God. He is being prepared by God for his future ministry, and he is sowing into his own ministry of helps. Moses was the man of God to conquer the Sinai desert, to prepare a way in a waste howling wilderness. He was the man to lead Israel out of the bondage of Egypt, to confront the powers of Pharaoh and to conquer the Sinai, but he was not the man to conquer the Promised Land. With all of his abilities, experiences and anointing, he was never able to possess Canaan's land. Had Joshua not faithfully served Moses, he would not have received the divine commission and possessed the land. It was Joshua who, in the end, proceeded to fulfil the commission once given to Moses.

The honor of divine commission is the fullness of the heart's submission.